Backyard Animals
Moose

Nick Winnick

www.av2books.com

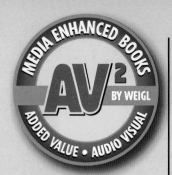

BOOK CODE

T889109

AV² **by Weigl** brings you media enhanced books that support active learning.

AV² provides enriched content that supplements and complements this book. Weigl's AV² books strive to create inspired learning and engage young minds for a total learning experience.

Go to **www.av2books.com**, and enter this book's unique code. You will have access to video, audio, web links, quizzes, a slide show, and activities.

Audio
Listen to sections of the book read aloud.

Video
Watch informative video clips.

Web Link
Find research sites and play interactive games.

Try This!
Complete activities and hands-on experiments.

Due to the dynamic nature of the Internet, some of the URLs and activities provided as part of AV² by Weigl may have changed or ceased to exist. AV² by Weigl accepts no responsibility for any such changes. All media enhanced books are regularly monitored to update addresses and sites in a timely manner. Contact AV² by Weigl at 1-866-649-3445 or av2books@weigl.com with any questions, comments, or feedback.

Published by AV² by Weigl
350 5th Avenue, 59th Floor
New York, NY 10118
Website: www.av2books.com   www.weigl.com

Library of Congress Cataloging-in-Publication Data

Winnick, Nick.
 Moose / Nick Winnick.
    p. cm. -- (Backyard animals)
Includes index.
 ISBN 978-1-60596-946-6 (hardcover : alk. paper) -- ISBN 978-1-60596-947-3 (softcover : alk. paper) --
ISBN 978-1-60596-948-0 (e-book)
1. Moose--Juvenile literature. I. Title.
QL737.U55W56 2010
599.65'7--dc22

                              2009050263

Printed in the United States of America in North Mankato, Minnesota
1 2 3 4 5 6 7 8 9 0 14 13 12 11 10

042010

WEP264000

Editor Heather C. Hudak   **Design** Terry Paulhus

Every reasonable effort has been made to trace ownership and to obtain permission to reprint copyright material. The publishers would be pleased to have any errors or omissions brought to their attention so that they may be corrected in subsequent printings.

Photo Credits
Weigl acknowledges Getty Images as its primary photo supplier for this title.

Contents

Meet the Moose

Moose are large, plant-eating **mammals**. They have a long head and body, with four spindly legs. Long, thick fur keeps moose warm and dry. Their fur can be light brown, black, reddish, or gray in color. A moose that has lighter-colored leg fur is said to have "stockings."

Male moose grow antlers, like deer or elk. When fully grown, moose have the largest antlers of any animal in the world.

Moose live all across northern Europe and Russia, and in nearly all of Canada's forests. In the United States, moose can be seen in much of New England and near the Rocky Mountains, in Utah, Colorado, and Wyoming. Alaska is home to the greatest number of moose in the United States.

The largest moose antlers were discovered in Alaska in 1897. They measured 79 inches (200 centimeters) from tip to tip.

Some small animals feed on moose antlers that have been shed.

All about Moose

Moose are the largest members of the deer family and some of the largest animals in North America. The largest moose live in Alaska. They can be as tall as 7 feet (2.1 meters) at the shoulder.

Moose are ungulates. These are animals that walk on hoofs that grow from the tips of their toes. There are two types of ungulates. The first kind has an odd number of toes. Rhinoceroses and horses are examples.

The second kind of ungulates have an even number of toes. Moose belong to this group, along with their close relatives, deer and elk. Pigs, giraffes, and hippopotamuses are other examples of even-toed ungulates.

Moose sometimes dive for food, but they mostly eat plants that grow near the surface of the water.

Types of Moose

Alaskan Moose

- Lives throughout Alaska and parts of the Yukon, Canada

Western Moose

- Lives in northern Michigan, Wisconsin, Minnesota, North Dakota, and Canada

Shiras Moose

- Lives along the Rocky Mountains, in Utah, Colorado, Wyoming, Montana, Idaho, and Washington, and north into the Canadian Rockies

European Moose

- Lives in northern Europe, from Norway to Siberia

Moose History

The moose's earliest known relatives lived in **Eurasia** about 20 million years ago. From there, they moved to Europe and the Americas. Present-day moose came from an animal in Europe called *Libralces gallicus*. It lived about two million years ago.

Broad-fronted moose lived in Eurasia during the last Ice Age. These huge animals had wide skulls and weighed up to 3,000 pounds (1400 kilograms). Their antlers were up to 10 feet (3 m) long.

At the end of the last Ice Age, the most common moose in North America was the stag moose. It looked like a tall moose with the face of an elk. The stag moose became **extinct** about 10,000 to 11,000 years ago.

Some people believe the stag moose became extinct due to competition for food from other types of moose.

In many parts of Europe, moose are called elk. In North America, the word "elk" is the name given to another member of the deer family.

Moose Shelter

Moose prefer to live in northern areas or at high **elevations**. They are mainly found in forested areas. These include the foothills of North America's mountain ranges, forests in New England and **Acadia**, and the boreal forests of Canada and Alaska.

Moose enjoy being near water and are often seen in and around lakes, rivers, and **muskegs**. In fact, moose can swim well only a few days after they are born. In summer, moose cool off by wading in water.

Sometimes, moose will venture onto tundra. This is a type of land found in the northern parts of Canada and Alaska. It has a harsh climate, and only small plants grow in the frozen ground there.

Moose can move through snow so deep that predators, such as wolves, cannot follow them.

Moose are strong swimmers. They have been known to swim as far as 12 miles (19 kilometers) in one trip.

Moose Features

Male moose grow a set of horns on both sides of their head. These horns are called antlers. While the antlers grow, they are covered by a thin layer of skin and soft fur called velvet. The velvet contains blood vessels that give the antlers the nutrients they need to grow. Each winter, moose shed their antlers. They grow another set, called a rack, in the spring. Antlers have many uses. Males grow antlers to attract females or to fight off other males during mating season. Antlers have a flat shape that is called "palmate" because they look like the palm of a hand. This shape helps moose hear.

LUNGS
Moose can hold their breath underwater. They can dive for as long as one minute.

LEGS
A moose's legs need to hold up a great deal of weight. Moose have powerful legs with wide flat hoofs. The shape of the hoof spreads the weight of the moose so it can walk on snow or uneven ground.

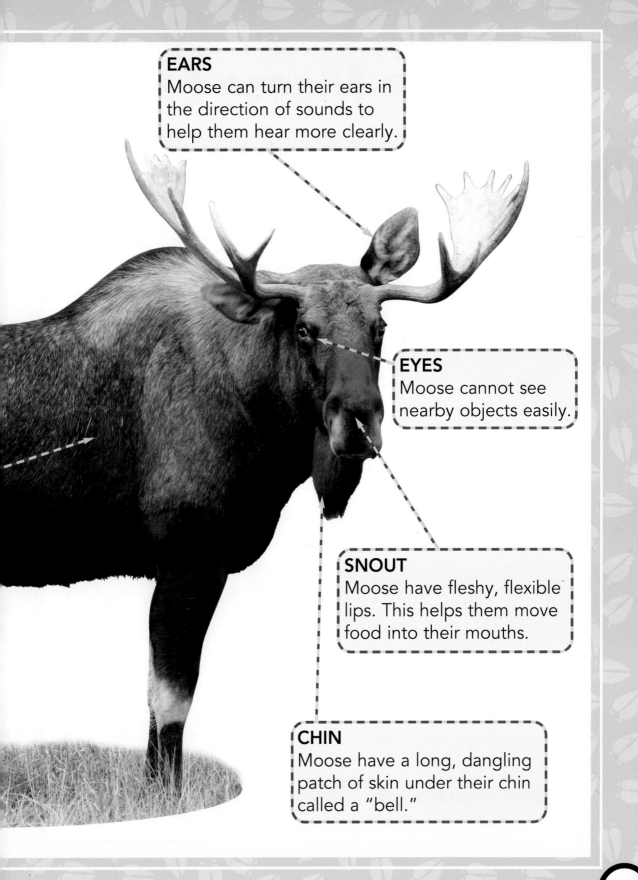

EARS
Moose can turn their ears in the direction of sounds to help them hear more clearly.

EYES
Moose cannot see nearby objects easily.

SNOUT
Moose have fleshy, flexible lips. This helps them move food into their mouths.

CHIN
Moose have a long, dangling patch of skin under their chin called a "bell."

What Do Moose Eat?

Moose are herbivores. This means that they only eat plants. A healthy adult moose needs to eat about 44 pounds (20 kg) of food per day. In North America, moose feed on 221 different types of plants.

In the Algonquin language, the word *moose* means "twig-eater." These animals were given this name because they survive the long winter months by eating twigs and small stems of trees and bushes.

In spring and summer, moose eat leaves and new **shoots**. Water plants are a favorite food of moose. These plants grow quickly and are easy to **digest**. Moose can often be seen diving in lakes and rivers to find water plants.

Male moose can weigh as much as 40 percent more than female moose.

Moose wade up to their shoulders in lakes and marshes to find food, such as lilies and weeds.

Moose Life Cycle

Mating season for moose takes place in the early fall. Males and females come together to mate in September and October. Young moose, called calves, are born about 230 days later.

Birth

Calves are born weighing about 35 pounds (16 kg). They grow very quickly, gaining as much as 2 pounds (1 kg) per day. Calves can swim within days of their birth. They can outrun a human before they are one week old.

Five Months

Calves follow their mother closely. For about five months, they will feed mainly on her milk. After five months, calves feed only on plants. Only about half of moose calves born in a year survive the first few weeks of life. Those that survive tend to live long into adulthood.

When it is time to give birth, female moose will look for a place far from other animals. Most females give birth to one calf at a time. However, twins are also common. Calves stay with their mother for about one year before living on their own.

Adult

Moose are considered mature when they can mate and produce their own calves. Moose can mate as early as 16 months old. Most moose grow to their full size by the time they are five years old. Full grown, male moose can weigh between 600 and 1,600 pounds (272 to 727 kg). Most female moose are smaller. They weigh between 500 and 1,300 pounds (227 and 590 kg).

Encountering Moose

Moose live far from humans, deep within rugged forests. Despite their large size, moose can move very quickly and quietly through dense forest. In fact, they can run as fast as 35 miles (56 km) per hour.

Most moose are gentle animals, but they can be dangerous. Female moose may charge if they are protecting their calves. During mating season, male moose, called bulls, can also be **aggressive**.

In rare cases, bulls have been known to charge at people, cars, horses, and even trains. Due to their large size, moose can easily hurt a person. For this reason, it is best to watch them from a safe distance.

Fascinating Facts

Moose that have been fed by people come to expect food. They might attack the next person they come across if no food is offered to them. For this reason, it is illegal in many places to feed moose.

Before resting, moose walk a complex path through the forest. This makes it difficult for predators to follow them.

Myths and Legends

Perhaps the best-known moose in the world is Bullwinkle. Bullwinkle and his friend Rocky the Flying Squirrel starred in their own cartoon show from 1959 to 1964.

Bullwinkle and Rocky would take part in many adventures as they tried to stop the plans of the evil Boris Badenov and his sidekick Natasha Fatale. Sometimes, Bullwinkle tried doing magic tricks to please his audience. In 2000, the adventures of Bullwinkle were made into a big-screen movie.

Rocky and Bullwinkle have been aired on television in more than 100 countries.

The Red Moose

The Algonquin people have many stories about moose.

At one time, the Algonquin were starving. They could not find much food on their lands. One day, a great red moose appeared before the youngest girl of the group. The moose told the girl to follow him into a swamp. She did as he asked.

At last, the moose led the girl to a place rich with wild grains and game. Thanks to the red moose, the girl was able to lead her people to a place where they could find food. They lived in this place for **generations**.

Frequently Asked Questions

How long do moose live?

Answer: Nearly half of all moose are **preyed** on by bears or wolves within six weeks of birth. Moose that reach adulthood can live as long as 15 years.

Do moose have any enemies?

Answer: Bears, wolves, cougars, and, sometimes, coyotes hunt moose. Newborn moose are at the highest risk. Adult moose are in the greatest danger from wolves during the winter, when deep snow may keep a moose from running away. However, their large size and antlers allow moose to defend themselves from predators.

Do moose live in groups?

Answer: Moose live alone. Male and female adults only meet during mating season. Young moose leave their mother after one year.

Words to Know

Acadia: former French settlement; parts of Eastern Canada and the state of Maine

aggressive: ready or likely to attack

digest: broken down in the stomach of an animal and used for nourishment

elevations: height above sea level; higher places tend to be colder, even in areas that are usually warm

Eurasia: a land mass that combined Europe and Asia

extinct: no longer living any place on Earth

generations: the period of time it takes for children to grow up and have children of their own

mammals: animals with warm blood that give milk to their young

muskegs: swamps or bogs in North America containing a great deal of moss

preyed: hunted by an animal for food

shoots: new plant growth

Index

Log on to www.av2books.com

AV² by Weigl brings you media enhanced books that support active learning. Go to **www.av2books.com**, and enter the special code inside the front cover of this book. You will gain access to enriched and enhanced content that supplements and complements this book. Content includes video, audio, web links, quizzes, a slide show, and activities.

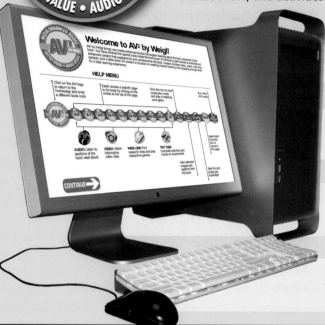

Audio
Listen to sections of the book read aloud.

Video
Watch informative video clips.

Web Link
Find research sites and play interactive games.

Try This!
Complete activities and hands-on experiments.

WHAT'S ONLINE?

Try This! Complete activities and hands-on experiments.	**Web Link** Find research sites and play interactive games.	**Video** Watch informative video clips.	**EXTRA FEATURES**
Pages 6-7 Identify types of moose.	**Pages 6-7** Find out more about moose features.	**Pages 4-5** Watch a video describing moose.	**Audio** Hear introductory audio at the top of every page.
Pages 12-13 List six important features of the moose.	**Pages 8-9** Learn about moose during the Ice Age.	**Pages 10-11** See a moose in its natural habitat.	
Pages 16-17 Compare the similarities and differences between a moose calf and an adult moose.	**Pages 10-11** Play an interactive moose game.	**Pages 14-15** Watch a video about a moose eating.	**Key Words** Study vocabulary, and play a matching word game.
Page 22 Test your moose knowledge.	**Pages 18-19** Find out fascinating facts about moose.		**Slide Show** View images and captions, and try a writing activity.
	Pages 20-21 Read more stories about moose.		**AV² Quiz** Take this quiz to test your knowledge